Conversations from the Classroom

A Public School Teacher Tells All
(Well, Almost)

Mary Crabapple

the three
tomatoes
Book Publishing

Published November 2022
ISBN: 979-8-9856298-9-7

For information address:
The Three Tomatoes Book Publishing
6 Soundview Rd.
Glen Cove, NY 11542
www.thethreetomatoespublishing.com

Cover and interior design: Susan Herbst
Cover image: Shany Muchnik via Shutterstock
Interior illustrations: Volha Hlinskaya, Olleg, and kbeis
via Shutterstock and iStock Photos

Dedication

To my children, parents, grandparents, teachers, co-teachers, paraprofessionals, friends, and family–including those who are not certified teachers who have taught me so much—
and of course to my students.
I love you all.

And to Cheryl Benton, our amazing editor, and publisher, who brought out the stories to give some lessons in laughs.

And please don't eat markers. Gelato is so much better!

You better watch out you better not cry.
You better not pout I'm telling you why.
I see you when you're texting, I know when you're asleep.
I know when you've been bad or good
so be good for goodness sake.

Even though I don't like this class, it's better than Zoom.

You should know that I can whisper softly sitting next to my bestie, but I have to shout to her across the room if you separate us.

They can hear my teacher voice in the next classroom.
Why can't you?

Why do I have to learn to spell when I have spell check on my phone?

You have to at least be able to spell well enough
so spell check can recognize your word.

I'm happy to be in detention so I can be alone
and look at my phone.

No, I'm not giving you my cell number for your mom to text me.

My mom said I should just ignore people who give me a hard time. Well, that's you.

I told my mom you are going to teach us how to curse and
write. She said you were going to teach us cursive writing.
I think she's wrong.

My computer was hacked, and the hacker
took my homework.

I'm sorry, is my teaching interrupting your talking?.

When you said we could read the book of our choice,
you didn't say it couldn't show naked people.

Just because your finger fits in your nose,
doesn't mean you have to pick it.

Your debate class is really helping me argue with my parents.

Can you teach us how the Kardashians became billionaires?

If I knew how the Kardashians became billionaires,
do think I'd be standing here?

When is bring our pets to school day?
I like my dog better than anyone here.

Of course, the classroom feels cold.
You're wearing shorts in January.

When is spring break? I'm so tired of school.

36 days, 8 hours, 43 minutes, and 10 seconds
until spring break.

Is sense of humor one of the five senses?

I have to go to the bathroom; my penis is getting big.

I know you say your child has a 180 IQ,
but I hate to tell you, he still bites his classmates.

Yes, I plagiarized but it was my sister's idea.
She said you wouldn't know and now we both know
she's the bad one.

Unless there's another teacher under the table,
you need to come out and join us.

If you won't let us use our phones,
how are we supposed to do our math?

I'm turning off my phone right now. Really, I am.

I'm not saying your son is a bad student.
He's gifted at making mistakes.

I'd really like to learn how to be a social blogger.
That would get me a better job with more pay
than this history crap.

All this talk about grammar is hurting my head.

Can you change math class to how to buy
a winning lottery ticket? Really, they both use numbers.
This is a good idea.

If I knew how to buy a winning lottery ticket,
would I be standing here?

Thanks for asking what we want to learn this year.
Can you teach me how to get Dylan to notice me
and be my boyfriend?

If you were more entertaining,
I wouldn't fall asleep at my desk.

If you're going to sleep in class, please don't snore and drool on the desk.

Why do we have to read Romeo and Juliet?
The movie version on Netflix is so much better.

There's a new cool app… it's called talking face to face.

Can I go to the bathroom?

I don't know. Can you, or may you?

I talk to everyone. So moving my seat won't help.

I couldn't do homework because I have soccer practice, piano lessons, and play dates. My mom says it's important to be well rounded and she didn't have time to do my homework.

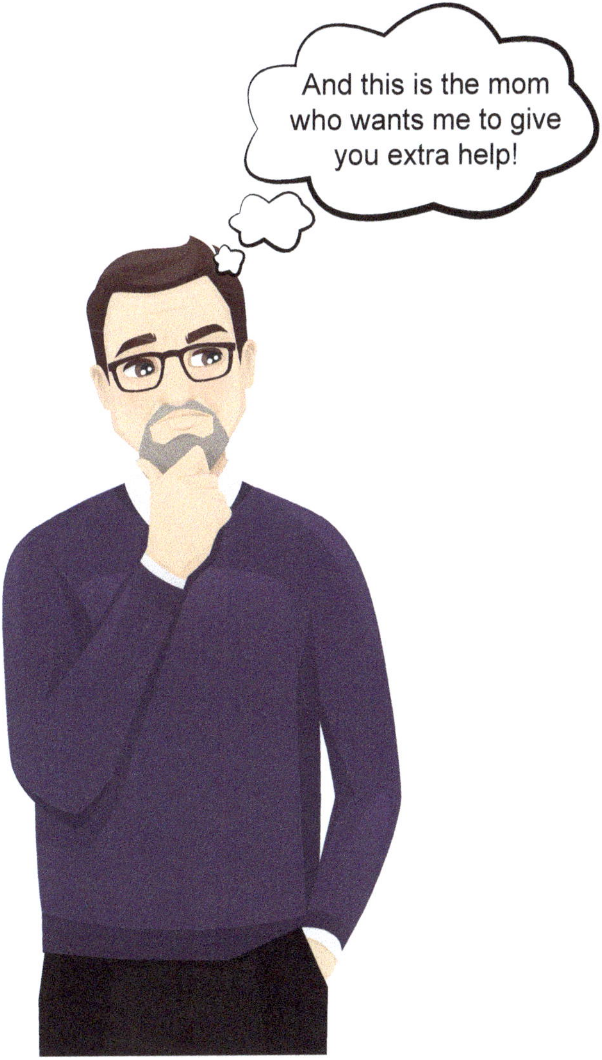
And this is the mom who wants me to give you extra help!

I already told you I'm going to be a movie star.
Enough with the math already.

I didn't think it would happen, but I really did learn a lot from you this year.

Mary Crabapple, (not her real name), has been an elementary school teacher in New York City for over twenty years. She has two master's degrees, two children, and two cats.

She decided to write this book under a pen name because she loves her students and would never say or think the critical teacher perspectives she shares in this book. And she thought it best to keep her identity confidential.

But "Mary" would like to give everyone a good laugh.

And part of the proceeds from this book will help her buy school supplies when students eat the pencils, and she needs more money to buy them new ones.